JAMAICA

AF767580

PEP

Language Arts

Performance Task

GRADE 4

Practice Papers

hachette LEARNING

The Publishers would like to thank the following for permission to reproduce copyright material.

Photo credits

t = top, b = below, l = left, r = right, c = centre, b/g = background

p.6: © SAMUEL/stock.adobe.com; p.7: © Vectorvstocker/stock.adobe.com; p.20: (t) © Gijsbert Hanekroot/Alamy.com, (b) © dpa picture alliance/Alamy.com; p.21: (l) © Janusz Pienkowski/Shutterstock.com, (l) © Prachaya Roekdeethaweesab/Shutterstock.com, (c) © Georgios Kollidas/stock.adobe.com, (c) © Everett Collection/Shutterstock.com, (c) © Prachaya Roekdeethaweesab/Shutterstock.com, (r) © vkilikov/stock.adobe.com, (r) © Prachaya Roekdeethaweesab/Shutterstock.com; p.26: © paladjai/stock.adobe.com; p.28: © Derariad/stock.adobe.com; p.33: © paladjai/stock.adobe.com; p.37: (l) © Drazen/stock.adobe.com, (l) © yaroslav1986/stock.adobe.com, (c) © Nancy Pauwels/stock.adobe.com, (r) © Krakenimages.com/stock.adobe.com, (r) © Pixel-Shot/stock.adobe.com; p.41: © paladjai/stock.adobe.com; p.42: (bg) © Eric Laudonien/stock.adobe.com, (l) © Joel/stock.adobe.com, (r) © JaeJun/stock.adobe.com; p.46: © paladjai/stock.adobe.com; p.49: (tl) © fotobild40/stock.adobe.com, (tr) © Superlenny/Shutterstock.com, (bl) © Marc Stephan/stock.adobe.com, (br) © Nenad Basic/stock.adobe.com; p.53: (tl) © Thidarat/stock.adobe.com, (tr) © SAMUEL/stock.adobe.com, (bl) © kreygscott/stock.adobe.com, (br) © Viktar Malyshchyts/stock.adobe.com; p.55: © Andriy Medvediuk/stock.adobe.com; p.56: © Towfiqu Barbhuiya/stock.adobe.com; p.63: © volff/stock.adobe.com; p.64: © Tartila/stock.adobe.com; p.65: © Tartila/stock.adobe.com; p.71: © udaix/stock.adobe.com; p.77: © eyetronic/stock.adobe.com; p.78: © Cisek Ciesielski/stock.adobe.com; p.81: © nezezon/stock.adobe.com, © zelimirzarkovic/stock.adobe.com.

p. 36: 'Sensational Senses' © Gillian Craig; p. 63: 'Water an Island's Treasure' © Susan Feller; p. 65: 'Water is good for us' by Stella Gray © Jamaica Observer; p. 78: *A High Wind in Jamaica* by Richard Hughes © Penguin Random House.

We have used all reasonable efforts to correctly credit all licensed material in this book. If your material has been miscredited please contact us so that we can amend the credit for future editions.

Acknowledgements

Although every effort has been made to ensure that website addresses are correct at time of going to press, Hachette Learning cannot be held responsible for the content of any website mentioned in this book. It is sometimes possible to find a relocated web page by typing in the address of the home page for a website in the URL window of your browser.

Hachette UK's policy is to use papers that are natural, renewable and recyclable products and made from wood grown in well-managed forests and other controlled sources. The logging and manufacturing processes are expected to conform to the environmental regulations of the country of origin.

To order, please visit www.HachetteLearning.com or contact Customer Service at education@hachette.co.uk / +44 (0)1235 827827.

ISBN: 9781036005160

First published in 2026 by Hachette Learning (a trading division of Hodder & Stoughton Limited),
An Hachette UK Company
Carmelite House
50 Victoria Embankment
London EC4Y 0DZ

www.HachetteLearning.com

The authorised representative in the EEA is Hachette Ireland, 8 Castlecourt Centre, Dublin 15, D15 XTP3, Ireland (email: info@hbgi.ie)

Impression number 10 9 8 7 6 5 4 3 2 1

Year 2030 2029 2028 2027 2026

Cover photo © GoodStudio- stock.adobe.com

Illustrations by Hyphen S.A./Konstantina Kyratzidou

Typeset by Hyphen S.A.

Printed and bound in Great Britain by Bell & Bain Ltd, Glasgow

A catalogue record for this title is available from the British Library.

FSC www.fsc.org
MIX
Paper | Supporting responsible forestry
FSC™ C104740

Contents

How to use this book

Think about successful athletes. Athletes learn about their sport, and they practise and train hard to become excellent performers.

You can excel at communication by learning how to identify the purpose and audience for communicating and then training yourself to answer different types of questions.

You are going to work through **Practice paper 1** with your teacher. This will help you to:

- Read questions carefully and work out what type of answer to give.
- Learn how you can get good results even if your answer is different from everybody else's.
- Understand what the different ratings mean and see how you can improve your rating.
- Reflect on your own work to help you see what you did well and what you can improve on in the next task.

Each task in this book has three supporting features.

Before you start ...

This section helps you to think carefully about questions and what it is you are being asked to do. There are different activities for each task.

Hints

These are given in the task itself to help you think about the questions and how you should answer them. As you progress, there will be fewer hints in the tasks.

Reflection

This section encourages you to think about your own learning and how you can improve on it.

Practice paper 1 also has a section called **How do you know how well you did?**

In this section you will see possible answers to the questions and what rating they were given. The aim of this section is to show you what you need to do to get the best possible results.

Practice paper 1

Always check that you have everything you need before you start.

This task has 2 parts:

- Part 1 has 5 questions.
- Part 2 has 1 question.

For both parts you must read **Source 1** and **Source 2**.

You will need a pencil and an eraser.

Answer all the questions in each part in the spaces provided.

→ Before you start …

Look at these students' responses for the following question: What are the different musical styles that make up Jamaican culture? Both students have the right answer, but Annika gets a better grade than Nadia. Can you see why?

Nadia's response	Annika's response
Jamaica has many musical styles, like mento, ska and reggae. Mento is Jamaican folk music from the past.	Jamaica has a rich and diverse tradition of musical styles, like jazz, mento, ska and reggae. These styles have developed over time and have been influenced by other cultures.

Nadia uses simple language, such as, "Jamaica has many musical styles" and "Mento is Jamaican folk music from the past." Annika uses more complex language, such as, "Jamaica has a rich and diverse tradition of musical styles …".

Nadia's answer is short and focuses on the main points, such as the different musical styles that make up Jamaican culture. Annika's answer is longer and includes more information, such as the origins and characteristics of the different musical styles.

Look at the instruction words and phrases in the Knowledge boxes on the next page. Which Knowledge box goes with Nadia and Annika's responses?

Write either **Recalling information**, **Skills and concepts**, **Strategic thinking** or **Extended thinking** under their name below. Think about what each instruction means in the Knowledge boxes before you answer the question.

Nadia

Annika

Depth of Knowledge

Recalling information	Skills and concepts	Strategic thinking	Extended thinking
Remember, recall, recognise or locate basic details, ideas. There is one correct answer.	Explain, show relationships, use your skills and what you know to make decisions about what to do and how to do it. There is one correct answer.	Explain your thinking and give reasons for your answers. There are different answers and different ways to find the answers.	Plan, think and put ideas together to solve a problem. There are many possible answers and ways of solving the problem.

Look at the end of the test to check the Knowledge box that goes with Nadia and Annika's responses.

Part 1

ICT link: You could record the poem on a phone or tablet to listen back to how the words sound.

Our musical heritage

SOURCE 1

Mango Time

I don't drink coffee or tea – mango time
I don't care how nice it might be – mango time
In the heat of the mango crop
When the fruit is ripe and ready to drop
Wash your pot, turn it over – mango time

The Terpentine is large and sweet – mango time
Robin Mango is so sweet – mango time
Number Eleven and Hairy-skin too
Pack the basket and ram them in
Because the basket must be full – mango time

Let's go on a mango walk – mango time
For it's just to talk – mango time
Let's jump on the big donkey
Let's ride it without stopping
Let's enjoy the harvest – mango time

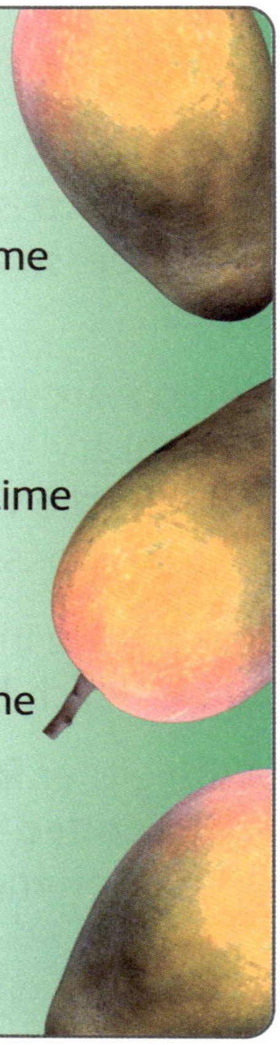

Music is often used to celebrate important events in Jamaican culture. For example, music is often played at weddings, funerals and other celebrations. To answer the questions, you will need to read the text and find information about the meaning of words.

SOURCE 2

Music and Celebrations

Jamaica has a lot of musical styles that make up its rich culture. Jamaicans listened to jazz from the 1940s. Then the mix of old musical styles produced mento music in the 1950s. By the 1960s calypso, jazz and mento together produced ska music which everyone loved. After this, reggae became very popular in the 1970s. Therefore, music has been a big part of the Jamaican people's culture and heritage.

Music and dance together are also important in Jamaican culture, and this can be seen in the carnivals and other celebrations of the island. People get very excited in the buildup to **these events**. It is not just **parades, parties and festivals** that create a thrill of anticipation, but also waiting for the seasons to collect the different ripened crops, especially the mango. Folk songs of Jamaica such as *Mango Time* celebrate **this harvest time** which makes Jamaicans so happy. The variety of Jamaican folk music displays the life of Jamaican people and their societies. There are folk songs for every stage of life such as marriage, birth and death. There is a folk song for all the main events in life.

There are songs for work, play, happiness and hope. There are also songs that make fun of people and songs that are sad. These are all part of Jamaica's culture and heritage.

Read the statements. Then look back at the Mango Time text above before selecting your answer.

Question 1

Choose one or more statements from (A), (B), (C) or (D) which could involve people collecting mangoes.

(A) Don't care how nice it may be

(B) Pack the basket and ram them in

(C) Let's go on a mango walk

(D) Let's enjoy the harvest

This is another way of asking you to think about what mango time means to the speaker.

Question 2

The speaker says, "I don't drink coffee or tea – mango time". Why do you think the speaker says this?

____

____

An adjective is a word that describes a noun, in this case, a mango.

Verbs can be used to describe an action. What actions happen during Mango Time?

How do you feel after you finish washing up?

Question 3

Use the information in the song *Mango Time* to answer questions **a** to **d**.

a What words in the song describe the noun mango?

____

b What mangoes are mentioned in the song?

____

c Describe some of the things people do during mango time.

____

____

d What do you think the phrase, "Wash your pot, turn it over" means?

____

____

Question 4

For each statement tick ✔ whether the information is from **Source 1**, **Source 2** or **Both sources**. Tick only one box for each statement.

	Statement	Source 1	Source 2	Both sources
1	When the fruit is ripe, it is ready to drop.			
2	Dancing to music is popular in carnivals, parades and festivals in Jamaica.			
3	The folk song *Mango Time* expresses the joy of the mango harvest.			
4	Folk songs are used to celebrate different stages and events in life.			

Question 5

Look at **Source 2** and answer the following questions:

a Name three musical styles that Jamaicans enjoyed before the 1970s.

Find the words "these events" in the text and read the sentence that comes before these words.

b What do "these events" refer to?

Think about what the word "thrill" means, then look at activities that the overall phrase is linked to.

c What does the phrase "thrill of anticipation" reveal about Jamaicans' attitude to music and culture?

Part 2

How we celebrate with music

Question 6

Write a letter to a cousin who lives in another country about the role of music in Jamaica's culture and heritage. In your letter, you must first describe the different kinds of music and their link to celebrations. Then, explain how the *Mango Time* song and other folk songs are used for various celebrations in Jamaica.

Look at the words "first", and then "second", in the writing prompt. This directs the order of events and will help you follow the sequence of your writing.

Pre-writing

a Highlight the key words in question 6. These are the words that let you know what you are supposed to do.

b Look at the words you have highlighted and make notes about the following:

- Audience – Who are you writing to?

____

- Purpose – What is the reason for writing?

____

____

- Verbs – What verb is used to indicate the purpose of writing?

____

- Topic – What is the writing about?

____

- Content – What are the points to support your topic?

____

____

____

When you write your letter, remember to use details in your own words from **Source 1** and **Source 2** to support your explanation.

Writing

Use the notes you have made to write your letter.

Practice paper 1 Self-evaluation

How do you know how well you did?

Here is the Knowledge box that goes with Nadia and Annika's responses:

Nadia: Recalling information
Nadia's response lists musical styles of Jamaica. This is useful and accurate. However, she does not explain any relationships between the musical styles or provide any insights into their development.

Annika: Skills and concepts
Annika explains how musical styles evolved and links them to other cultures. This shows deeper conceptual thinking.

Therefore, Nadia's response is "Recalling information" and Annika's response is "Skills and concepts".

Now that you have worked through Practice paper 1, you are going to look at some answers that students gave to see how they were rated. Then you can rate your own answers using this scale.

Remember: There are often many ways to show understanding. Your response doesn't have to look exactly like the examples to be valid.

1 Beginning	2 Developing	3 Proficient	4 Highly proficient
The student starts to share ideas. May need support to develop answers or explore the topic more fully.	Answers show some evidence that the student partly understands the concepts.	The student clearly understands the concepts and provides solid examples or explanations.	Answers show that the student understands all the concepts very well and may have found the task quite easy.

Different thinkers may reach proficiency in different ways – by writing, drawing, speaking or explaining in their own words.

We will look at answers to the four different levels of questions.

Recalling information	**Skills and concepts**	**Strategic thinking**	**Extended thinking**

Recalling information

Question 1

Choose one or more statements from (A), (B), (C) or (D) which could involve people collecting mangoes.

(A) Don't care how nice it may be

(B) Pack the basket and ram them in

(C) Let's go on a mango walk

(D) Let's enjoy the harvest

b Pack the basket and ram them in

c Let's go on a mango walk

d Let's enjoy the harvest

2 Developing	3 Proficient	4 Highly proficient
*Selection of either **b**, **c** or **d**.*	*Selection of any 2 from **b**, **c**, **d**.*	*Selection of all three – **b**, **c** and **d**.*

*The selection of **b** shows that the student associates the verbs "pack" and "ram" with collecting mangoes. The verb "pack" and the strong verb "ram" means fill the basket with mangoes and squeeze them tightly.*

*The selection of **c** shows that the student associates "mango walk" with going for a walk to pick mangoes.*

*The selection of **d** shows that the student associates the word "harvest" with collecting mangoes.*

Strategic thinking

Question 2

The speaker says, "I don't drink coffee or tea – mango time". Why do you think the speaker says this?

The speaker does not like tea or coffee.	• The speaker is so excited about mango season that they would rather eat mangoes than drink coffee or tea. • The speaker associates mangoes with a sense of community and celebration, while coffee and tea are more associated with everyday life.

1 Beginning	3 Proficient
The student is starting to make connections, but has not yet shown how the answers relate to specific words or phrases in the text.	*The student has demonstrated that they understand the concepts of "pack" and "ram", "mango walk" and "harvest".*

Recalling information

Question 3

Use the information in the song *Mango Time* to answer the questions **a** to **c**.

a What mangoes are mentioned in the song?

The Robin mango.	The Turpentine, Robin Mango, Number Eleven and Hairy-skin.
1 Beginning *The student mentions the name of the mango that has the adjective "Robin" directly in front of the noun "mango".*	3 Proficient *Other than "Robin mango" the other adjectives ("Turpentine", "Number Eleven" and "Hairy-skin") are understood to be the names of mangoes because they act as an adjective that comes before the noun mango.*

b Describe some of the things people do during mango time. (Strategic)

Walk, talk, jump on a donkey.	During Mango Time people go on mango walks to pick ripe mangoes, they ride donkeys with baskets full of mangoes and eat mangoes. They enjoy collecting mangoes during the harvest.
1 Beginning *This response simply lists actions which lacks description.*	3 Proficient *This response is proficient because it is complete and supported. It answers the question in a complete and informative way.*

c What do you think the phrase, "Wash your pot, turn it over" means?

The phrase "Wash your pot, turn it over" means get the pot ready to collect mangoes.	The phrase "Wash your pot, turn it over" in the song means that people should wash and dry their pot and get ready to collect mangoes. It is also a Jamaican expression that means you should be prepared for something.
2 Developing *This response shows some evidence that the student understands the concept of getting the pot ready for mango time.*	4 Highly proficient *The student offers a response in the context of the song and indicates how this phrase is used in everyday life.*

Extended thinking

Question 4

For each statement tick ✔ whether the information is from **Source 1**, **Source 2** or **Both sources**. Tick only one box for each statement.

	Statement	Source 1	Source 2	Both sources
1	When the fruit is ripe, it is ready to drop.	✔		
2	Dancing to music is popular in carnivals, parades and festivals in Jamaica.		✔	
3	The folk song *Mango Time* expresses the joy of the mango harvest.			✔
4	Folk songs are used to celebrate different stages and events in life.		✔	

Statement 1	Statements 2 and 4
1 Beginning *The student correctly identifies **Source 1**. The statement is close to the exact words in the text.*	2 Developing *The student correctly identifies **Source 2**. The statements are similar to the words in the text.*

Statement 3
3 Proficient *The student connects the verb "enjoy" from **Source 1** and "celebrate" from **Source 2**.*

Skills and concepts

Question 5

Look at **Source 2** and answer the following questions:

a Name three musical styles that Jamaicans enjoyed before the 1970s.

Reggae plus any two musical forms: Jamaicans enjoyed reggae, jazz/calypso/mento/ska before the 1970.	Any three of the following: Jamaicans enjoyed jazz, calypso, mento and ska before the 1970s.
3 Proficient *The student is able to identify two musical forms that Jamaicans enjoyed before the 1970s but is not able to determine that reggae emerged in the 1970s.*	4 Highly proficient *The student is able to search through paragraph one and identify the popular musical forms that Jamaicans enjoyed from the 1940s to the 1960s.*

b What do "these events" refer to?

music and dance	carnivals and other celebrations
1 Beginning *The student talks about music and dance in general but doesn't yet show how they connect to real events or celebrations.*	3 Proficient *The student associates events with occasions where Jamaicans include music.*

c What does the phrase "thrill of anticipation" reveal about Jamaicans' attitude to music and culture?

Jamaicans enjoy their music and culture.	Jamaicans eagerly look forward to the festivals and celebrations that include music and are part of the culture. This shows that they enjoy both the music and what it represents of the cultural heritage.
3 Proficient *The student correctly connects the phrase to the attitude of enjoyment.*	4 Highly proficient *The student does not link the phrase to the attitude of enjoyment but also explains how the enjoyment of music and culture are tied together.*

Question 6

Write a letter to a **cousin** who lives in **another country** about the **role of music** in **Jamaica's culture and heritage**. In your letter, you must first **describe the different kinds of music and their link to celebrations**. Then, **explain how the *Mango Time* song and other folk songs are used for various celebrations in Jamaica**.

Format for friendly / informal letter which includes:

- punctuated sender's address and date
- salutation
- paragraphs in the body
- punctuated closing and signature

Content:

- Paragraph 1 – greet cousin and state reason for writing
- Paragraph 2 – include the different types of music mentioned in **Source 2** and how they are used in celebrations and events in the country
- Paragraph 3 – explain how music, especially folk songs are used to represent the culture and various celebrations

1 Beginning	2 Developing
The letter shows some early effort, but it doesn't yet follow a clear letter format. The person receiving the letter might not be named, and the ideas may not be grouped into paragraphs yet. The student has tried to include information about Jamaican music from **Sources 1** and **2**, but the ideas need more organisation to be fully clear. The letter may still need a closing and signature. There are several grammar or punctuation slips, which can be improved with support.	The student uses a letter format even if incorrect. The recipient is correctly identified. There is some effort to use paragraphs but may be inconsistent. The letter does not follow a logical sequence. The letter has a closure and signature. There are many grammatical errors.

3 Proficient	4 Highly proficient
The student uses the correct letter format but may have punctuation errors. The recipient is correctly identified. The letter is separated into paragraphs but has not included all the information as instructed. The letter has a closure and signature. There are some grammatical errors.	The student has written a near perfect letter - the correct letter format with appropriate punctuation. There is the use of paragraphs that follow a logical sequence. The tone is appropriate for the task. The letter has a closure and signature. There are no more than three grammatical errors.

Reflection

Complete this flow chart.

My strengths

____

____

Evidence of my strengths

____

____

My goals for the next performance task

____

____

My plan to reach the goals

____

____

Practice paper 2

This task has 2 parts:

- Part 1 has 6 questions.
- Part 2 has 1 question.

For both parts you must read **Source 1**, **Source 2** and **Source 3**.

Answer all the questions.

Draw or write your answers to all the questions in the spaces provided.

→ Before you start …

There are different levels of comprehension questions. Each level requires a different type of answer. Write the number in the blank boxes, to match the comprehension level on the left with the skills on the right.

Comprehension levels	Skill levels
The writer and you: the answer is not in the text. You will have to link what you know with what is in the text.	**1. Recalling information:** remember, recall, recognise or locate basic details, ideas. There is one correct answer.
Easy to find answer: the answer is in one place.	**2. Skills and concepts:** explain, show relationships, use your skills and what you know to make decisions about what to do and how to do it. There is one correct answer.
In your view: the answer is not in the text. You will have to draw on what you know.	**3. Strategic thinking:** explain your thinking and give reasons for your answers. There are different answers and different ways to find the answers.
Think and search: you need to pull the answer together from several places.	**4. Extend thinking:** Plan, think and put ideas together to solve a problem. There are many possible answers and ways of solving the problem.

Part 1

☆

ICT and Mathematics link: You could make a music survey! Use Google Forms to ask your family or friends which Bob Marley song they like best. Draw a graph to show the results.

Famous Jamaicans

SOURCE 1

Bob Marley

Bob Marley, the singer and songwriter, died in 1981. Marley's music was a mix of reggae, ska and rocksteady, which was also the music of other Jamaican singers. Today, reggae is one of the most popular sorts of music in the world because of Marley and this has helped to make Jamaica a popular tourist destination.

Marley's family was poor when he was born, so he had to work hard to overcome these challenges in his life. As Marley grew up, he never gave up on his dreams, and his music became a source of hope and joy for many Jamaicans with similar backgrounds. Bob Marley's music is still popular today. He is a true musical and cultural icon, and his legacy will live on for generations to come, so he is an important person in Jamaican history.

SOURCE 2

Usain Bolt

Usain Bolt is thought to be the greatest sprinter of all time and he has made Jamaica famous for producing the fastest man in history with a time of 9.58 seconds. His eight Olympic and eleven World Championships gold medals have made Jamaicans feel proud of their country.

In addition to his athletic accomplishments, Bolt is also a talented musician. Like other famous vocalists before, his music is a blend of reggae, dancehall and pop. His songs are about his life as a runner, but he also sings about other things like love, happiness and motivation.

Bolt's music is popular with people of all ages. His first album, Country Yutes, reached number one in the Jamaican reggae chart. His second album, Usain Bolt Presents: 9.58 Riddim, was also a success.

SOURCE 3

Should they be awarded the Order of National Hero?

The definition of a national hero in Jamaica is a person who was born in Jamaica or lived there and did something very good for the country. The Order of National Hero is a special award that the government of Jamaica gives to these people.

Usain Bolt was born in Jamaica and is a famous Jamaican athlete, although he recently retired from athletics. He motivates many young people to follow their dreams. He is a role model for athletes of all ages because he is dedicated to hard work and excellence.

Bob Marley was also born in Jamaica and died in 1981. He was a famous Jamaican musician who helped to promote Jamaica's culture and values around the world. He showed young musicians that you can do anything you want if you believe in yourself and work hard, so he was also a role model for musicians. He wrote music about love, peace and unity. He helped to make Jamaica a country that people want to know more about.

Both Bolt and Marley have made Jamaicans proud of their culture and heritage. Bolt's Olympic wins have made Jamaica a household name, and Marley's music has helped to put Jamaica on the map as a cultural destination. Both men are not official national heroes, but in the eyes of many Jamaican people, they should be given this award as their contributions to Jamaican culture and heritage will be remembered for generations to come.

Where do you need to look in **Source 1** to find the words that show the music that Bob Marley performed?

Question 1

a As stated in **Source 1**, what kind of music did Bob Marley make?

Look at where the word "challenges" is used in **Source 1**. Is the word linked with something that is easy or difficult?

b What was one challenge that Bob Marley faced in his early life?

Think about the meaning of the words "tourist" and "destination" and how Bob Marley's music contributed to that for Jamaica.

c How did Bob Marley's music help to make Jamaica a more popular tourist destination?

The phrase "known for" means the reason someone or something is famous or recognised.

Question 2

a What is Usain Bolt known for according to **Source 2**?

"Accomplishments" is another way of saying "achievements". Which achievement does Bolt mention in his music album?

b In **Source 2**, which of Bolt's two albums shows that he is proud of his athletic accomplishments?

____

____

____

What does someone do to make you feel proud?

c How has Usain Bolt made Jamaica proud?

____

____

____

ICT link: You could learn more about Usain Bolt online (with an adult), then plan and record a short podcast. Use safe sites such as YouTube Kids.

Question 3

According to the texts, many Jamaicans think Bob Marley and Usain Bolt should be national heroes. Give one reason from **Source 1** for Bob Marley and one reason from **Source 2** for Usain Bolt.

You can use your own words as well as information from the texts, but all the reasons must relate to the text.

____

____

____

____

____

____

____

Question 4

Read the sentence from **Source 1**, then choose one answer (A), (B), (C) or (D) from **Source 2** that expresses the same idea.

Source 1

Marley's music was a mix of reggae, ska and rocksteady which was also the music of other Jamaican singers.

Source 2

(A) Bolt is also a talented musician.

(B) Like other famous vocalists, his music is a blend of reggae, dancehall and pop.

(C) His songs are about his life as a runner, but he also sings about other things like love.

(D) Bolt's music is popular with people of all ages.

Question 5

a For each statement, **a** to **h** put a tick ✔ if the text is about the similarities, or if it is about the differences between Bob Marley and Usain Bolt.

b For each statement **a** to **h** identify the word that shows the similarity or the difference. The first one is done for you as an example.

		Similar	Different	Word
a	Bob Marley was a musician, while Usain Bolt is an athlete.		✔	while
b	They have both inspired people around the world.			
c	Bob Marley's music is more political than Usain Bolt's music.			
d	Bob Marley died in 1981, but Usain Bolt is still alive.			
e	Bob Marley and Usain Bolt are both Jamaicans.			
f	They have similarly achieved great things in their fields.			
g	They are equally role models for young people.			
h	Bob Marley's music was a mix of reggae, ska and rocksteady, however Usain Bolt's music is a blend of reggae, dancehall and pop.			

Question 6

a What do you think the future holds for Bob Marley's music and reputation?

____

____

Part 2

Do we need more heroes?

Question 7

Bob Marley and Usain Bolt are famous Jamaicans who have done great things for Jamaica. Some people think that they should be made national heroes.

Using information from **Sources 1**, **2** and **3**, write a letter to the local newspaper to persuade and explain two reasons why you think Bob Marley and Usain Bolt should be awarded the Order of National Hero.

- Your letter should be short and easy to understand.
- You can use the following information to guide you in your letter:
  - Bob Marley was a musician who sang reggae music.
  - Usain Bolt is an athlete who is the fastest man in the world.
  - Both Bob Marley and Usain Bolt have made Jamaica famous.
  - Both Bob Marley and Usain Bolt have inspired young people.

Pre-writing

a Highlight the key words in question 7. These are the words that let you know what you are supposed to do.

b Look at the words you have underlined and make notes about the following:

- Audience – Who are you writing to?

____

- Purpose – What is the reason for writing?

____

____

- Verbs – What verb is used to indicate the purpose of writing?

____

- Topic – What is the writing about?

____

- Content – What are the points to support your topic?

____

____

____

____

____

____

Think about using different expressions. Instead of writing "Bob Marley was a famous musician," I could write "Bob Marley made Jamaica famous."

Instead of just describing facts, I could write "Bob Marley's music inspired people … ".

Is there any information from the answers in part 1 that I could use in the letter?

Writing

Use the notes you have made to write your letter.

Reflection

Answer these questions once you have completed the task.

- What evidence shows that I have achieved my aims?
- What did I do well?
- What can I improve on?

Practice paper 3

This task has 2 parts:

- Part 1 has 4 questions.
- Part 2 has 1 question.

For both parts you must read **Source 1**, **Source 2** and **Source 3**.
Read through all the questions in this task and answer all the questions.
Write your answers in the spaces provided.

→ Before you start ...

You need to read the source materials carefully or you will not be able to answer the questions correctly. There are several things that you should pay attention to as you read the texts.

- What kind of writing is it? This will help you to decide the writer's purpose.
- What is the main idea? How do I know?
- Who is the intended audience? What evidence can I find to confirm this?

Part 1

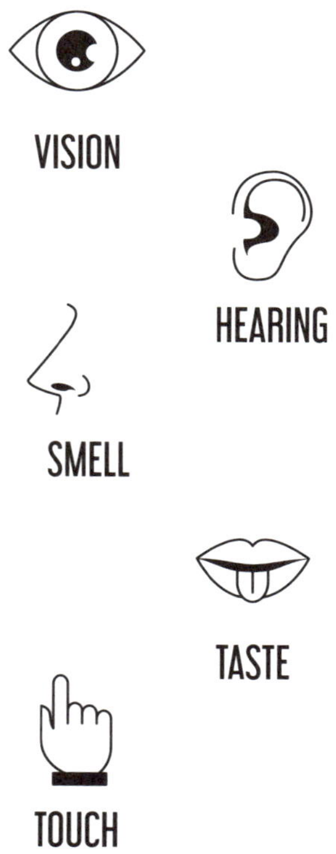

The value of our sense

SOURCE 1

Our Sense Organs: the Skin, Nose and Tongue

Such soft skin that covers us all. It protects us from the rays that fall.

We feel pain when we encounter danger, such as a sharp object from a stranger.

Breathing in the scent of a rose, the nose can also smell our woes.

Our nose helps us to smell smoke from a burning fryer and warns us if there is a wildfire.

The tastebuds love honey on the tongue but can also detect when something is wrong.

The tastebuds love honey on the tongue but can also detect when something is wrong.

Our tongue tastes food that is spoiled over days, so we know to throw it away.

Our senses help us to see, hear, touch, smell and taste, keeping us safe – should we need to escape.

To sum up, the skin, the nose and the tongue are a team and work together like a dream.

They warn and defend us to keep us alive, so we should protect them if we want to survive.

SOURCE 2

The Environment and Our Senses

Our environment can have a big impact on our senses. The air we breathe, the water we drink and the food we eat can all affect our sight, hearing, smell, taste and touch.

Pollution

Sight – Pollution in the air can make it difficult to see things clearly. Tiny dust particles can irritate the eyes and make them water. Smoke and dust which is smog can also make things less visible making it difficult to drive or move about safely.

Hearing – Noise pollution is often not taken seriously, but loud noises can damage our hearing. Noise pollution can come from traffic, construction and even loud music. It can cause hearing loss, and in some cases affect your balance.

Touch – Extreme temperatures, such as heat or cold, can damage our skin and affect our sense of touch. Chemicals generated from gasses in the air can irritate the skin and cause dangerous health problems.

Smell – Powerful smells can also affect our sense of smell and make our eyes water. Strong smells, such as smog or rotting rubbish, can irritate the nose and alter our sense of smell making it difficult to smell other things.

Taste – Our taste is affected by the quality of the water we drink and use to wash our bodies. Contaminated water not only makes our food taste off but is also dangerous for our health.

Protection

We can all do our part to protect our environment and our senses. Here are some tips:

- Reuse and recycle.
- Reduce water and energy usage and conserve these resources.
- Plant trees.
- Limit your use of chemicals that pollute the air and water.
- Only buy goods from businesses that are environmentally friendly.
- Participate in environmental projects.
- Spread the word to others about protecting our environment.
- Change daily habits, such as walking or biking instead of driving. This will reduce your carbon footprint which is the impact you have on the environment.

By caring for our environment, we can help to protect our senses and our health.

SOURCE 3

Dear Local Council,

We would like to express our concern about the environment and how it is affecting our senses. As you know, our senses are important for our safety and well-being. They help us to see, hear, smell, taste and touch the world around us.

The environment can affect our senses in many ways. Pollution in the air can make it difficult to see, hear, smell, taste and touch. For example, air pollution can cause smog, which can make it difficult to breathe and see. Noise pollution can damage our hearing. Extreme temperatures can damage our skin and make it difficult to feel things. And contaminated water can make our food taste bad and even make us sick. There are plenty of things that can be done such as:

- Reduce pollution by making stricter laws against pollution of the environment.
- Plant more trees which will help clean the air.
- Protect our parks and green spaces for people to enjoy.
- Promote recycling to help reduce waste.
- Educate people about the importance of protecting the environment.

We should all do our part to protect our environment and our senses, but we need your help. We are looking forward to your response.

Sincerely,

Kings High School – Class 4

This is another way of asking you to explain what you understand to be the overall message of Source 1.

Look at **Source 1**.

Question 1

a What is the main idea of the text?

b List two ways the skin protects us.

Look back at the line that contains the phrase. Would you say the writer has a positive or negative view of the way these sense organs work together?

c What does the phrase, "work together like a dream" reveal about the writer's view of these three sense organs?

Question 2

How do the skin, nose and tongue work together to keep us safe?

Look at **Source 2**.

Question 3

Read **Source 2**, *The Environment and Our Senses*. Then, use the text features to answer the following questions:

Text features are headings, subheadings and bold words which help you find the information you are looking for quickly.

a How does pollution affect our sight?

b How does noise pollution affect our hearing?

c How do extreme temperatures affect our touch?

d How do strong smells affect our smell?

e How does contaminated water affect our taste?

____

f What are some things we can do to protect our environment and our senses?

____

Homophones are words that have the same sound but have different meanings and spellings. For example, the words "bare" and "bear" sound the same, but they have different meanings. "Bare" can mean empty while "bear" can mean an animal.

Question 4

Complete the activity on homophones.

Look at the words below which come from **Source 3**. Write a homophone for each word. The first one is done for you as an example.

a to / two

b our / ________

c see / ________

d hear / ________

e there / ________

f be / ________

Part 2

Saving our environment and our senses

Look at **Source 3**.

Question 5

You are a Grade 4 student at Kings High School. Read **Source 3** for the letter your class wrote to the local council.

Now write a letter to a **friend** who lives in **another country** about how the environment is affecting our senses and what they can do to help. In your letter:

- Explain the concerns that your class has about the environment affecting our senses.
- Share the suggestions that your class made to the local council for protecting the environment and our senses.
- Encourage your friend to tell others to protect our senses.

ICT and Science link: You could use tools like Canva or Google Slides to make an infographic on how pollution affects our senses.

Writing

What exactly is the task? I must read **Source 3** carefully, so I know what to write about to my friend.

What is the purpose of writing? I need to explain how important it is to protect our senses and our environment.

What evidence do I need to use from the sources? I should underline all the ideas in **Source 3** that I can use in my letter.

Reflection

Use your answers to the task to analyse your strengths and weaknesses.

- What areas are you good at?

- Which areas require more work?

- What work will you do?

Practice paper 4

This task has 2 parts:

- Part 1 has 3 questions.
- Part 2 has 1 question.

For both parts you must read **Source 1** and **Source 2**.

Answer all the questions.

Write or draw your answers in the spaces provided.

→ Before you start ...

Instruction words or phrases help you to use information to answer questions or complete tasks correctly. Write the number in the boxes provided, to match the instruction words and phrases on the left with the skills on the right.

Instruction words	Skills
Use evidence	**1. Recalling information:** Remember a fact or way of calculating what you learned and write it down. There is one correct answer.
Explain	
Circle	**2. Skills and concepts:** Use your skills and what you know to make decisions about what to do and how to do it. There is one correct answer.
Select	
List	**3. Strategic thinking:** Explain your thinking and give reasons for your answers. There are different answers and different ways to find the answers.
Match	
How do you know?	**4. Extend thinking:** Plan, think and put ideas together to solve a problem. There are many possible answers and ways of solving the problem.
What is ...?	

Part 1 Living through our senses

Science link: You could pick one sense and think about how things like smoke, noise or dirty water might affect it. Draw or write what you find out!

SOURCE 1

Sensational Senses by Gillian Craig

1 What will your wonderful eyes see today?
Will they see ocean and sand in a bay?
Will they see shells or a star or a dime?
Open your eyes, what can you see this time?

2 What will your magical ears hear today?
Will they hear trains slowly clacking away?
Will they hear feet stepping or a bell's chime?
Open your ears, what can you hear this time?

3 What will your marvellous hands touch today?
Will they touch grass or concrete or hay?
Will they touch feathers, will they touch slime?
Stretch out your hands, what can you touch this time?

4 What will your fabulous nose smell today?
Will it smell flowers in a lovely bouquet?
Will it smell laundry, or is it teatime?
Lift up your nose, what can you smell this time?

5 What will your excellent tongue taste today?
Will it taste lemon? Can it taste sorbet?
Will it taste chilli, or cookies or lime?
Stick out your tongue, what can you taste this time?

SOURCE 2

My Grandmother

I unlocked my grandmother's bedroom door quietly. It was dark in the room, but I knew I should not draw the curtains, so I shuffled my way around carefully until I reached my grandmother's dressing table. I saw the trinket box which contained jewellery that she wore, but this was now my mother's. I opened the box slowly and it all flooded in. I remember how I used to sit on my grandmother's lap and pull gently at the sparkling lights that hung from her ears and neck. Oh, now I wish, just once more, I could smell that faint sweet musk as I nuzzled closely whilst gazing at the shimmering dangling lights.

Look at **Source 1**.

Question 1

a Match pictures A to E to stanzas 1 to 5 of the poem.

A	B	C	D	E

Stanza ______	Stanza ______	Stanza ______	Stanza ______	Stanza ______

Read the poem in Source 1 to find words that suggest whether the poet is angry, happy, sad or indifferent to his or her senses.

b Select the adverb from the poem and explain how it is linked to one of the senses.

____

c How do you think the poet feels about his or her senses? Use two examples from stanza 1 to stanza 5 to support your point.

____

____

d Explain the message that the poet wants to share with readers.

____

____

Look at **Source 2**.

You will need to read the first part of **Source 2** and look at the clues about how he entered the room to find your answer.

Question 2

Read the experience that is described in **Source 2** and then answer the following questions.

a Does the boy have permission to be in his grandmother's room? How do you know?

____

b What do you think has happened to his grandmother? Use evidence from the passage to support your answer.

____

____

c Circle the word that best describes the meaning of "nuzzled"?

(A) slept (B) snuggled

(C) snored (D) snoozed

d Circle the phrase that best describes the meaning of "flooded in"?

(A) A feeling of loneliness was present.

(B) Memories came rushing to mind.

(C) Sadness came rushing to the surface.

(D) A sense of laughter was present.

Look at **Sources 1** and **2**.

Question 3

a List all the senses that are mentioned in both texts.

____

____

b Both sources refer to a shining object. What is it and how is it described in each source?

Source 1 ____

Source 2 ____

Part 2

Can you picture it?

Question 4

Task:

Highlight the key words in the writing prompt below. Are there any more key words you could highlight to help you write clearly?

Your school is hosting a writing competition for Grade 4 students to see who can use their expressions to create a picture in the reader's mind.

Write a description about your most memorable experience as your entry for the competition. Include descriptions of the sights, sounds, touch, smells and tastes of the experience.

Your description should have clear paragraphs that help the reader to picture the experience.

Pre-writing

a Highlight the key words in question 4. These are the words that let you know what you are supposed to do.

b Look at the words you have underlined and make notes about the following:

- Audience – Who are you writing to?

____

- Purpose – What is the reason for writing?

- Verbs – What verb is used to indicate the purpose of writing?

- Topic – What is the writing about?

- Content – What are the points to support your topic?

Writing

Use the notes you made to write your description.

Reflection

Can you answer "yes" to all of these questions?

If not, write down what you need to do to change your answer.

- Did I understand all of the questions?

- Did I know what to do to answer them?

- Did I follow the instructions correctly?

- Was my work clear and organised?

- Did I perform procedures accurately?

- Was I able to use my calculator efficiently?

- Did I explain and justify my answers when asked to do so?

Practice paper 5

This task has 2 parts:

- Part 1 has 4 questions.
- Part 2 has 1 question.

For both parts you must read **Source 1** and **Source 2**.
Make sure you have everything you need.
Read each question carefully before you answer it.

→ Before you start ...

Did you know that having a clear purpose for writing makes it easier to decide how to start writing, what to write and how you want readers to react?
A writer's purpose or intent can be to persuade or to inform or to entertain. Can you think of any others?

As you read **Source 1** and **Source 2**, try to find clues that reveal each writer's purpose.

Part 1

The beauty of the Jamaican Blue Mountains

ICT and Geography link: You could use Google Earth or an online map to find the Blue Mountains in Jamaica. Zoom in to spot rivers, forests or trails. What do you notice?

SOURCE 1

A Blue Mountains Vacation

Are you feeling drained? Do you need a holiday?

Then, do not delay. Visit the Blue Mountains of Jamaica right away!

Wake up to the crisp refreshing breeze and discover how Blue Mountain got its name as you gaze at the beautiful morning haze.

Let the sweet music of nature serenade you as you leisurely hike a stunning trail.

While you are there, find the historic towns and villages that play hide and seek among the valleys and peaks.

Learn about the culture of coffee that has grown in the mountains for centuries.

Enjoy the entertainment of singing, cooking and eating around a campfire.

Then camp under the stars at night.

The Blue Mountains are a great place to relax and escape the hustle and bustle of everyday life.

Book your trip today!

SOURCE 2

A UNESCO World Heritage Site – The Blue Mountains of Jamaica

The UNESCO World Heritage Site recognises the Blue Mountains as being outstanding in value to the country and therefore needs to be protected. The Blue Mountains are the longest mountain range in eastern Jamaica and are famous for the stunning blue haze above the mountain tops and their production of coffee.

The Blue Mountain coffee plant is one of the most valued in the world. The plant is grown high up in the mountains. The rich flavour and aroma of the coffee have convinced Japan of its quality as they purchase 90% of the annual crop of coffee beans. The Blue Mountains are also home to a variety of plants and animals which draw many tourists to the area.

The Blue Mountains host several rivers and streams, which provide the island with a significant source of water. This includes water for drinking, irrigation and hydroelectric power.

Development and climate change in the Blue Mountains is threatening the natural environment and the production of coffee. Climate change impacts the mountains' natural balance of the ecosystem.

Protecting the Blue Mountains is a priority for the wildlife that live on the island. The mountain range is a valuable natural resource and a source of beauty and pride for Jamaicans. So, it is vital to protect the colonies of ants, the swarms of insects, the clouds of butterflies and all the wildlife that support the area. Students should be educated in how to protect the Blue Mountains. This can be done by learning about them, so they can help to bring about change in activities that negatively impact the environment.

Look at **Source 1**.

Question 1

a Name two things that visitors to the Blue Mountains can enjoy.

____

b What is the purpose of the two questions at the beginning of the advertisement?

____

c According to the advertisement, how will visitors benefit from a trip to the Blue Mountains?

Think about what it means to play hide and seek. Can towns and villages really do that?

d Explain how the expression, “the historic towns and villages that play hide and seek among the valleys and peaks” help you to picture the landscape.

Look at **Source 2.**

a Why is the Blue Mountains a UNESCO World Heritage Site?

Collective nouns refer to a group of things. For example, for a group of lions we say, “a pride of lions”. Here are some more examples: a flock of birds, a school of fish, a pack of wolves, a herd of elephants.

b Who according to the passage, purchases most of Jamaica’s Blue Mountain coffee?

c Explain why the rivers in the Blue Mountains are important to Jamaica.

d Look at the last paragraph of the article and identify the collective nouns.

Look at **Sources 1** and **2**.

Question 3

a Which source is mainly about promoting tourism in the Blue Mountains of Jamaica?

Source ______________

b Which source is mainly about the importance of protecting the Blue Mountains?

Source ______________

Question 4

Describe two ways, one from each source, that the Blue Mountains of Jamaica can be promoted for tourism:

Source 1

____

____

____

Source 2

____

____

____

Part 2

ICT link: You could record a short video or audio message inviting Rhonda to Jamaica. Describe your favourite places and explain why she should visit them. Use a phone, tablet or computer.

Come to Jamaica!

Question 5

Your friend, Rhonda, from Barbados is coming to Jamaica for one week during the school holidays this summer. You are very excited and want to tell her all about Jamaica and all the beautiful places (beaches, mountains and rivers) you can visit in a friendly letter. Look at the template to help you organise your ideas. Here are some things to remember as you write your first draft:

- Use correct punctuation, including commas and capitals.
- Use collective nouns and vocabulary about the physical features of Jamaica.

Pre-writing

a Highlight the key words in question 5. These are the words that let you know what you are supposed to do.

b Look at the words you have underlined and make notes about the following:

- Audience – Who are you writing to?

____

- Purpose – What is the reason for writing?

____

____

- Verbs – What verb is used to indicate the purpose of writing?

____

- Topic – What is the writing about?

____

- Content – What are the points to support your topic?

____

____

____

____

(Your address)

(Today's date)

Dear, ______________________ (your friend's name)

(Introduction: Say who you are and why you are writing this letter.)

(Paragraph: Include the information that you would like to tell your friend.)

(Ending: Finish by thanking your friend for reading your letter.)

(A personal letter could end with a casual ending, such as Best wishes, and underneath this write your name.)

Writing

Use the notes you have made to write your letter.

Reflection

Complete this flow chart.

My strengths	Evidence of my strengths	My goals for the next performance task	My plan to reach the goals

Practice paper 6

This task has 2 parts:

- Part 1 has 5 questions.
- Part 2 has 1 question.

For both parts you must read **Source 1** and **Source 2**.

You will need a pencil and an eraser.

Answer all the questions in each part in the spaces provided.

→ Before you start …

You do not speak to your parents or other people in authority the same way you speak to friends. You should practise the same idea in your writing. Always know your audience so that you can use the appropriate tone and expressions. Who do you think are the audience in **Source 1** and **Source 2**?

Part 1

Jamaica is a gem

ICT and Social Studies link: You could use a computer or tablet to make a poster about Jamaica. Add pictures of beaches, mountains and rivers.

SOURCE 1

The Jamaican island's physical landscape

Jamaica's **landscape** is made up of a variety of physical features. The **mountains** are craggy and tall and are home to a plethora of plant and insect wildlife. The wildlife also lives in the lush green rainforests which is a place of many trees. **Caves** lay hidden in dark and quiet places underground. **Waterfalls** such as Dunn's River Falls originate from high places, and the **springs** such as Milk River Bath flows out of the ground. The long **river** of Rio Grande and the mangrove swamps of the Black River are just a few examples of the waters that **stream** from the mountains to the **sea**. The waters leave from the **shore** which is the part of the land that meets the sea. This shore leads into the not-too-distant **coral** reefs that surround Jamaica's edge of land known as the **coastline**.

SOURCE 2

Jamaica: The jewel in the Caribbean crown

From an array of spices, such as nutmeg, cinnamon and ginger to beautiful beaches, lush rainforests and tall mountains, Jamaica is the jewel in the Caribbean crown.

What you can do in Jamaica:

Visit the Dunn's River Falls and attempt to climb the cascading waterfall.

Wind through the rainforest while rafting on the Rio Grande River.

Hike to the top of Blue Mountain Peak, the highest point in Jamaica.

Relax on one of the many beautiful beaches, such as Negril Beach or Montego Bay Beach.

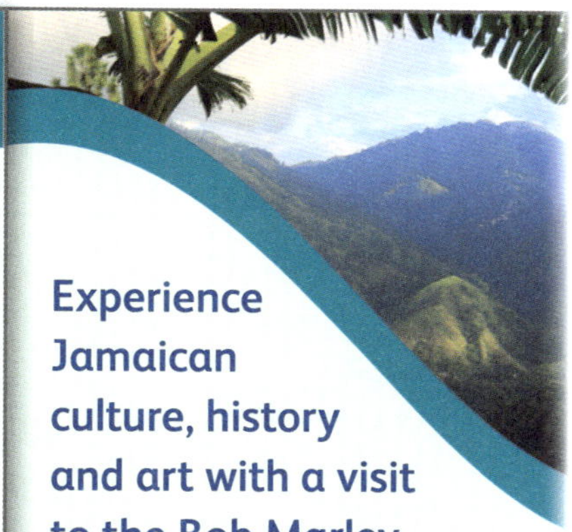

Experience Jamaican culture, history and art with a visit to the Bob Marley Museum or the National Gallery of Jamaica.

Experience the local cuisine and taste the jerk chicken, curry goat and ackee and saltfish.

Experience this beautiful island with something for everyone. So, what are you waiting for? Contact us today to book your trip!

Look at **Source 1**.

Question 1

a Based on the way it is used, the word "plethora" means the same or nearly the same as which of these words from **Source 1**?

Ⓐ variety Ⓑ place

Ⓒ example Ⓓ part

To justify means that you provide evidence to support your view or idea.

b Which sentence reveals the main idea in the passage? Justify your answer.

c According to the writer, describe the route that the water takes from the high places to the coral reefs?

d What difference does the writer point out between Dunn's River Falls and Milk River Bath?

e Complete the syllables table by writing the features of the Jamaican landscape in the correct column.

mountain rainforest caves waterfalls springs
river stream sea shore coastline

One syllable	Two syllables	Three syllables

If explicit information is directly stated in the text and implicit means the opposite of explicit, what is implicit information?

Question 2

a Identify the explicit and implicit information from **Source 1**. Write E to indicate explicit and I for implicit next to the information in the following table.

	Information	E or I
a	Jamaica's landscape is made up of a variety of physical features.	
b	Jamaica is a tropical island.	
c	The mountains are a source of water for the surrounding area.	
d	The mountains are rocky and tall.	
e	The rainforests are lush and green.	
f	The rainforests are home to a variety of plants and insect life.	
g	Caves are a mysterious and fascinating place.	
h	Caves lay hidden in dark and quiet places underground.	
i	Waterfalls such as Dunn's River Falls originate from high places.	
j	Waterfalls are a popular tourist destination.	
k	This shore leads into the not-too-distant coral reefs that surround Jamaica's edge of land known as the coastline.	
l	The shore is a popular spot for recreation.	

Look at **Source 2**.

Question 3

a What does the phrase, "the jewel in the Caribbean crown" reveal about the writer's view of Jamaica?

Remember, purpose means the same as intent or reason.

b What is the purpose of the photos in the advertisement?

c Why do you think the writer repeats the word "experience" so many times?

Look at **Sources 1** and **2**.

Question 4

a Which source is mainly about activities that you can do in Jamaica?

Source ____________

b Which source is mainly about Jamaica's physical landscape?

Source ____________

Question 5

Describe two ways, one from each source, that you can experience the culture of Jamaica.

Source 1

____

____

____

Source 2

____

____

____

Part 2

ICT and Mathematics link: You could make a digital pictograph to track how many Jamaican fruits you eat each day.

Eat what we grow!

Question 6

Your school is running an essay competition on Jamaican fruit. The purpose of the competition is to persuade the readers about the importance of eating Jamaican fruit and supporting the Jamaican fruit industry.

Look at the poster of four local fruits: passionfruit, mango, ackee and pineapple. Describe how these fruits could be included in a healthy diet. Provide evidence from the poster to support your claims.

The fruits from our land

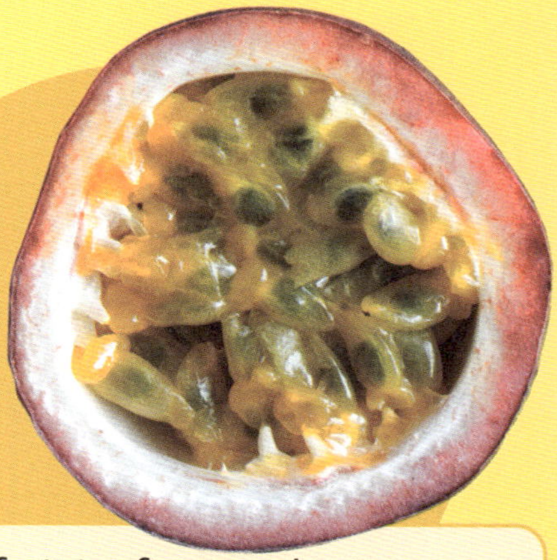

The passionfruit is often used in juices and desserts. It is a popular fruit in Jamaica. Passionfruit is a good source of vitamin C, potassium and fibre.

The mango is often used in desserts and smoothies. It is a popular fruit in Jamaica. Mango is a good source of vitamins A and C, as well as potassium.

Ackee is used in savoury dishes. It is a bright orange fruit and the national fruit of Jamaica. Ackee is a poisonous fruit unless it is cooked properly. When cooked properly, it has a creamy texture. It is often served with saltfish and is a good source of protein and fibre.

The pineapple is often used in desserts and smoothies. It is sweet and juicy, with a slightly tart aftertaste. It is a popular fruit in Jamaica and is grown all over the island. Pineapple is a good source of vitamin C.

Your essay should include the following:

- A brief description of three fruits, including their appearance, taste and nutritional benefits.
- An explanation of how at least one of the fruits could be included in a healthy diet.
- A concluding comment on the importance of eating Jamaican fruit and supporting home grown fruit from Jamaica.

Writing

Reflection

Analysing your mistakes can help you improve.

Consider any questions that you got wrong.

- Did you understand the question and know what to do? If not, what can you do about this?

- Would doing corrections help you? If so, redo the questions you got wrong.

Practice paper 7

This task has 2 parts:

- Part 1 has 5 questions.
- Part 2 has 1 question.

For both parts you must read **Source 1** and **Source 2**.
Remember to read each question carefully, then answer all of them in each part in the spaces provided.

→ Before you start ...

Read the information below which will help you do well in the PEP assessment.

- Circle or highlight all the instruction words.
- Underline any words that tell you to give a reason for your answers.
- Some questions are open-ended. That means there is more than one way to answer.
- It is important to explain your answer where possible.

Part 1 Water is life!

SOURCE 1

Cascade Hill Water Crisis

Cascade Hill is a small town on a neighbouring island where access to water for many homes is limited. Fortunately, the local school and hospital have running water, but there are some serious problems.

Problems

Recently, the water has become muddy and brown in colour. People have said it smells and it looks **polluted**. The local people are scared that the running water is **contaminated** and unsafe to drink.

The local school has stopped children from drinking the water because it probably contains **bacteria** that can cause **diseases**. This is causing problems during the school day with some children bringing water from home and others going without.

There is already an impact on local businesses which depend on the water supply. If the water is not safe to drink, these businesses will have to close, which will lead to job losses and economic problems. The water company has not responded to the complaints from the local people.

Drinking contaminated water will cause serious health problems for young children and the elderly who are more at risk of becoming sick.

Solutions

- Write to the government asking for urgent action to solve the problem.
- Boil all water used for drinking at home.
- Ask the local government to reduce the cost of bottled water from the shops.

SOURCE 2

Clean Water

Clean water is essential for drinking, cooking, farming and therefore living. However, over two billion people do not have access to safe drinking water (WHO, 2023). This should be unacceptable in the world today. This report will outline the reasons for a lack of access to clean water, the negative consequences of this and finally what can be done to improve access to clean water.

The reasons for a lack of access to clean water.

- An underdeveloped society with a poor infrastructure: These can be areas of natural disaster, drought or flooding. Often the government does not have enough money to manage these problems.
- Pollution: People dump waste and contaminate the water. The water is then unsafe to drink and can make people sick.
- Conflict: Limited access to water can cause war. Communities may fight over access to water if they do not have enough.

The negative effects of a lack of access to clean water.

- Disease: People catch diseases such as cholera and typhoid from drinking dirty water. The young and old are especially at risk.
- Poverty: Farmers cannot grow crops or raise animals without clean water. This can lead to hunger and death.

How to improve access to clean water.

- Invest in the community: Governments should build water pipes and wells to bring clean water to everyone.
- Reduce pollution: Organisations must stop dumping sewage and industrial waste in the water.
- Resolve conflict: Governments and organisations can work to solve conflicts over water.

Clean water is a basic human right. Everyone should have access to safe water.

Consider the overall meaning of the sentence. Review the words that come before and after the word you are trying to understand. Finally, use your knowledge of the world to make inferences about the meaning of the word.

Look at **Source 1**.

Question 1

The following words in bold are from **Source 1**. Work out the meaning of the word from the context of the sentence.

a The food was **contaminated** with bacteria, so it was not safe to eat.

____

b The factory's chemical waste **polluted** the river, killing many fish and making the water unsafe for swimming.

____

c The **bacteria** in the water made people sick.

____

d The **disease** is being spread by mosquitoes, so we must apply insect repellent.

____

Question 2

a Name two effects of the water crises on the people of Cascade Hill.

____

____

Look at the passage again, how does the writer want his audience to react?

b What do you think is the writer's purpose in **Source 1**? How do you know?

____

c Why do you think the writer mentions young children and the elderly?

____

Look at **Sources 1** and **2**.

Question 3

For each statement tick ✔ whether the information is from **Source 1**, **Source 2** or **Both sources**. Tick only one box for each statement.

	Statement	Source 1	Source 2	Both sources
1	a specific local water problem in a small town			
2	the impact on the health of the community			
3	the importance of clean water in general			
4	the global impact of the water problem			
5	understanding the water problem and the need to find solutions			

Question 4

a Identify the text features in the sources and complete the tables.

Source 1

Title	
Subheadings	
Bolded words	
Purpose of text	

Source 2

Title	
Subheadings	
Bolded words	
Purpose of text	

> Are there any similarities or differences in the way the text features are used?

b Look at your responses in the tables and answer the question: How do the text features in the two sources compare?

____

____

Look at **Source 2**.

Question 5

Complete the graphic organiser with the relevant details from **Source 2**, the report. The first part, the Hook and the first subheading have been completed as examples.

Introduction		
Hook: How will you grab the reader's attention? For example: Clean water is essential for drinking, cooking, farming and therefore living.	**Definition:** What is the Topic? Clean water	**Importance:** It is essential for living.
Body		
1st subheading The reasons for a lack of access to clean water.	**Reasons:** Underdeveloped society, poor infrastructure, natural disasters, pollution, conflict	**Importance:** It is important to identify the problems so we can find solutions.
2nd subheading	**Negative effects:**	**Results:**
3rd subheading	**Action required:**	**Results:**

Part 2

ICT and Science link: You could create a slideshow or short video to show the importance of clean water. Use photos, facts and voice-over. Share it to raise awareness.

Let's help a neighbour

Question 6

Your friend goes to the local school in Cascade Hill which is having serious clean water problems. Write a letter to the principal of your school explaining the situation in Cascade Hill.

- In your letter you should describe the water crisis in **Source 1** and refer to the global water crisis in **Source 2**. Use the information you wrote in the graphic organiser in question 5 to guide you.
- Express how fortunate your school is to have clean running water and how the children and people in Jamaica are protected from the problems described in **Sources 1** and **2**. Identify at least one problem from each source.
- Ask the principal for permission to run a fundraising event for the children's school in Cascade Hill.
- Conclude your letter by thanking the principal for considering the fund-raising and by writing that you look forward to their response.

Writing

Reflection

Use this scale to rate your work for each question.

Write the question numbers in the correct spaces in the table.

4 Excellent	3 Accomplished	2 Getting there	1 Trying

How can this table help you prepare for the next task?

Practice paper 8

This task has 2 parts:

- Part 1 has 5 questions.
- Part 2 has 1 question.

For both parts you must read **Source 1**, **Source 2** and **Source 3**.

Make sure you have everything you need.

Read each question carefully before you answer it.

→ Before you start ...

Look at these students' responses for the following question: Based on the text in **Source 1**, answer the question: What short-term solutions should the local people put in place to minimise the negative impact of the water crisis?

Both students have the right answer, but Annika gets a better grade than Nadia. Can you see why?

Nadia's response	Annika's response
Boil the drinking water at home. Buy clean water in a bottle from the shop.	If short-term solutions such as buying bottled water daily are too expensive, it is not financially possible. Therefore, the next best solution is to boil water at home and use a water filter if possible. The most important action is to protect the health and well-being of the person.

Nadia suggests simple solutions using basic language. Annika uses more complex language and explains her thinking such as, "If short term solutions such as buying bottled water daily are too expensive, it is not financially possible."

- Look at the instruction words and phrases in the Knowledge boxes on the next page. Which Knowledge box goes with Nadia and Annika's responses?
- Write either **Recalling information**, **Skills and concepts**, **Strategic thinking** or **Extended thinking** next to their name below. Think about what each instruction means in the Knowledge boxes before you answer the question.

Nadia ______________________________

Annika ______________________________

Depth of Knowledge

Recalling information	Skills and concepts	Strategic thinking	Extended thinking
Remember, recall, recognise or locate basic details, ideas. There is one correct answer.	Explain, show relationships, use your skills and what you know to make decisions about what to do and how to do it. There is one correct answer.	Explain your thinking and give reasons for your answers. There are different answers and different ways to find the answers.	Plan, think and put ideas together to solve a problem. There are many possible answers and ways of solving the problem.

Look at the end of the task to check the Knowledge box that goes with Nadia and Annika's responses.

Part 1

The gift of water

ICT link: You could use presentation software to turn the poem into a digital slideshow. Add background images, voice-over reading and water sound effects to bring it to life.

SOURCE 1

Water an Island's Treasure
by Susan Feller

Water defines us.

Water sustains us.

It reflects us, protects us,

Supports our animals and plants.

Water is solace and refuge,

Protection and threat.

And our water is endangered by

the very people it supports.

SOURCE 2

The water in our bodies

Our skin contains around 65% of water. Our brain comprises 75% water. The lungs are made up of 83% water and the kidneys and muscles are made up of 83% water. Finally, our bones are made up of 31% of water (Tuarez, 2022). Various studies claim that over 60% of body weight comes from water.

Therefore, people should consume enough water for the body to function correctly. The recommended daily amount of water required may differ for each person. The amount of water we need depends on the person's age, activity level and health as well as the climate.

https://healthierliving4you.com/much-water-consume-daily-basis/

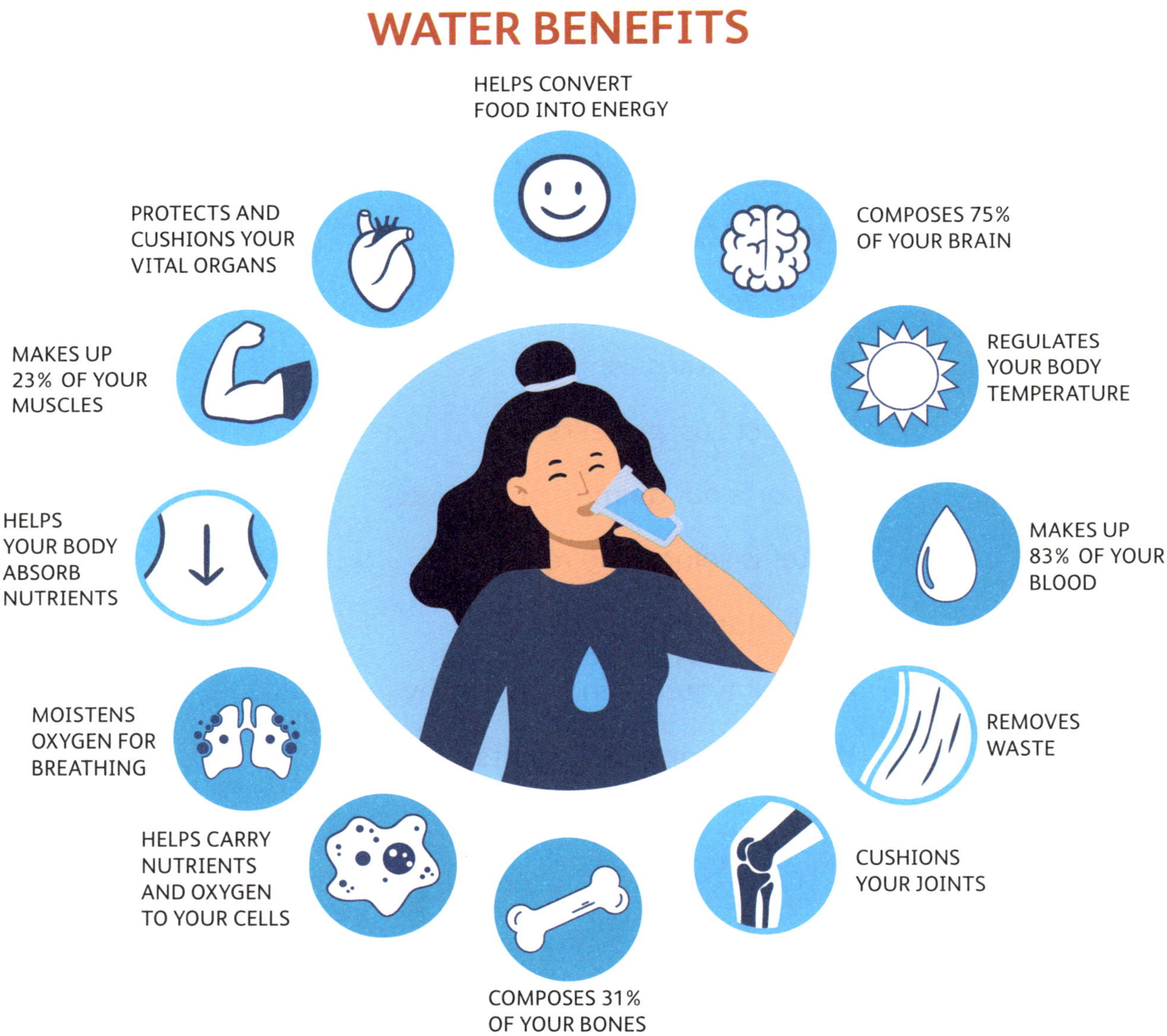

SOURCE 3

Water is good for us

Water is the most abundant substance in our body and is found in every organ, tissue and cell. Our body consists of approximately 70% or about ten to 12 gallons of water. We are able to survive for up to six weeks without food but can only survive approximately one week without water.

We lose water daily through urine, perspiration, bowel movements and even breathing. We need to replace this water as the body does not store an extra supply. The amount of water we need daily depends on several things, such as how active we are, our body weight, illness, pregnancy, sweating and level of exposure to dry air.

So, what does water actually do for us? For a start, it helps to keep our heart healthy. Blood is mostly water, so when we are properly hydrated our body will be thinner. This makes it easier for our heart to pump and so gives it less work. People who drink plenty of water are likely to have less heart problems.

Water plays a part in transporting oxygen to all the cells of our body. Our lungs are almost 90% water so adequate hydration will help keep our lungs moist and healthy. Water is vital for flushing toxins from our body. Keeping our kidneys properly irrigated can lessen the chance of kidney stones. It can help lower blood pressure and cholesterol. It keeps our skin looking healthy as it cleanses built-up toxins from our skin and makes our skin moist and hydrated. If we feel puffy and bloated it means we are not drinking enough water.

Question 1

Identify the category of the word in the boxes. Write noun, pronoun or verb below the word. One is done as an example.

Example

Water	defines	us
noun	*verb*	*pronoun*

a

Water	sustains	us

b

It	reflects	us	protects	us

c

Supports	our	animals	and	plants

d

Water	is	solace	and	refuge	protection	and	threat

Look at **Source 1**.

Question 2

a Work out the meaning of the word from the context of the sentence. One is done as an example.

! Example

After the earthquake, the water was not fit for **consumption**, so the government had to provide bottled water for the people during the crisis.

drinking

i He found **solace** in visiting his mother's grave.

____

ii People found **refuge** in the mountains when their town was flooded.

____

iii Due to global warming, increasing numbers of animals and plants are now **endangered** as they are dying due to changing weather patterns.

____

b Answer the following questions about the poem.

i What is the main idea of the text?

____

ii Why is, "our water endangered by the very people it supports"?

____

iii How does the text make you feel?

____

Question 3

What kind of images come to your mind when you answer the following questions? One is done as an example.

Example

How does water reflect us?

Water may reflect a wavering image of ourselves. It could also reflect my uncertainty as my image changes with the movement of the water.

Consider the title and each sentence of the poem. Then use your knowledge of the world to make inferences about the meaning of each sentence. Finally, based on your understanding, respond to the questions.

a How does water define us?

____

____

____

b How does water sustain us?

____

____

c How does water protect us?

____

____

Look at **Sources 2** and **3**.

Question 4

a According to **Source 2**, how much of our body is made up of water?

____

b How does **Source 3** support this claim?

____

c According to **Source 2**, how much water do we need to drink daily?

____

d How does **Source 3** support this claim?

____

Question 5

Which detail in **Source 2** supports the claim that the amount of water we need depends on several factors including our physical condition and the environment we live in? Circle the correct response.

(A) The lungs are made up of 83% water, and the kidneys and muscles are made up of 83% water.

(B) Various studies claim that over 60% of body weight comes from water.

(C) The amount of water we need depends on the person's age, activity level, health as well as the climate.

(D) Therefore, people should consume enough water for the body to function correctly.

Part 2

Drink up!

Question 6

Write an essay to explain the benefits of staying healthy and hydrated in preparation for your school's annual sports day. Use evidence from **Sources 2** and **3** to support the points you make in your essay. Use transitional words to help your sentences flow. Your essay must include an introduction, body and conclusion.

Writing

Reflection

Use your answers to the task to assess your own learning.

List the question numbers.

Rate your work on each question using this scale:

Below standard	On track	Above standard

Practice paper 9

This task has two parts:

- Part 1 has 6 questions.
- Part 2 has 1 question.

For both parts you must read **Source 1** and **Source 2**.

→ Before you start …

Read the information below which will help you do well in the PEP assessment.

Transitional words make writing flow from one idea to the next. They can be used within a paragraph and from one paragraph to the next to show order or sequence.

For example, transitional words are used to show time order or cause and effect.

- Some time/order transitions are, “firstly”, “next”, “finally”.
- Some cause and effect transitions are, “because”, “therefore”, “as a result”.

Part 1

Whims of the weather

Science link: You could look outside and observe the weather. Draw what you see and write one sentence to predict what the weather might be like tomorrow.

SOURCE 1

Weather

The gases that surround the Earth are called the atmosphere. The weather is created out of the atmosphere. The weather conditions include the outside temperature, precipitation, humidity, wind speed, rain, sun and snow. The weather varies during different seasons and across different countries.

The Earth's energy comes from the Sun. The atmosphere distributes this energy in the form of weather conditions around the Earth. The Earth's surface, which is the ocean or land, plays a role in the weather's condition as it absorbs and releases heat.

Meteorologists are weather scientists. They predict the weather using equipment that examines weather conditions. They also look for unexpected weather activity such as heavy rains which can cause life threatening flash floods. A flash flood is a rapid flooding of low-lying areas usually caused by heavy rainfall. Meteorologists warn people of extreme danger due to unexpected weather conditions.

The seasons are opposite in the northern and southern hemispheres. This is because when the Northern Hemisphere is tilted towards the Sun, the Southern Hemisphere is tilted away from the Sun. For example, in Argentina and Australia which is in the Southern Hemisphere, winter begins in June, but summer is in December. Jamaica has a tropical climate which means it is warm and humid for most of the year. However, other places, like Greenland, are cold and snowy all year.

Earth's Vital Areas
(Angle of Sun Rays)

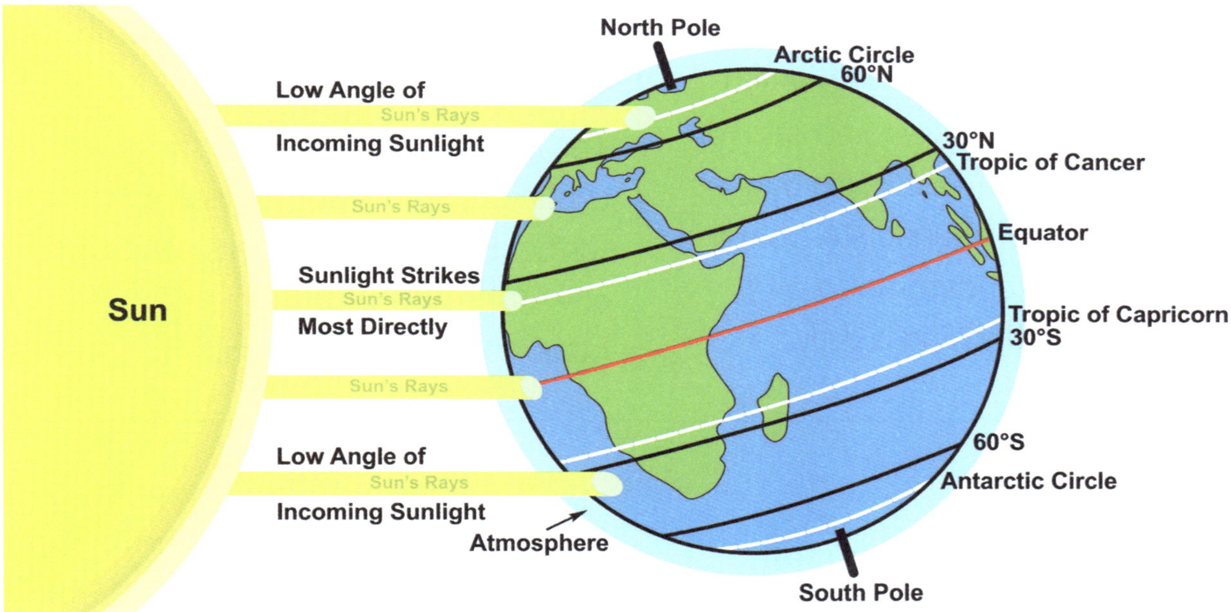

The weather impacts our daily lives as it affects what we can do and when we may be in danger. For example, if you are caught in a flash flood you could drown, and you would need to move to higher ground. You would not be able to drive through the floodwaters. You could get shocked by damaged electricity cables. You need to find refuge until it is safe for you to return to your home and daily life.

SOURCE 2

KINGSTON, Jamaica – The Meteorological Service has issued a flash flood watch for low-lying and flood-prone areas of St Elizabeth, Manchester, Clarendon, St Catherine, Kingston, St Andrew, St Thomas, Portland and St Mary effective until further notice.

Several buildings in St Andrew have been washed away and some minor roads in St Thomas are flooded. The police are also reporting landslides in Portland. The police are advising motorists to avoid these locations.

The meteorologist manager stated, "Satellite Data shows that moderate to heavy showers have been occurring since mid-morning. The forecast is for light to moderate showers to continue tonight. However, thunderstorms will affect most parishes tomorrow, therefore flash flooding is likely."

The Meteorological Service urged fishers to exercise caution as they believe conditions could become life threatening.

If the flash flood watch upgrades to a flash flood warning, residents need to secure their property, protect their livestock and crops if possible, and they should ensure they have a supply of clean water.

The Meteorological Service said it will continue to monitor this system. For further information, citizens can dial 116 or visit the website at **http://metservice.gov.jm.**

Look at **Source 1**.

Question 1

Match the headings A to E with the correct paragraphs 1 to 5.

A	Weather and its dangers	
B	The Sun, the Atmosphere and Earth's Surface	
C	Climate differences around the world	
D	What is weather?	
E	The science of weather	

Look at **Sources 1** and **2**.

Question 2

a What does a meteorologist do? Give one example from **Source 1** and one from **Source 2**. For each example, include the source number.

Source 1 ______________________________

Source 2 ______________________________

> You must base your answer on a logical reason.

b In your opinion, what's the most beneficial part of a meteorologist's job?

____

Look at **Source 2**.

Question 3

Answer the questions about the report.

a Name three places that have been affected by this flooding.

____

b Describe the damage that has been caused by this flooding.

____

____

c What advice have the police given to people?

____

> A fact is supported by evidence. An opinion is based on what a person believes.

Question 4

a Write which sentence is a fact and which is an opinion.

i Satellite data shows that moderate to heavy showers have been occurring since mid-morning.

____

ii However, thunderstorms will affect most parishes tomorrow, therefore flash flooding is likely.

____

b Identify another fact and an opinion from the text. Do not use the ones identified above.

Fact ____

____

Opinion ____

____

Look at **Sources 1** and **2**.

Questions 5

a A sentence from **Source 1** says, "Meteorologists warn people of extreme danger due to unexpected weather conditions." Which two sentences from **Source 2** best supports this sentence? Circle your answers.

(A) The Meteorological Service has issued a flash flood watch for low-lying and flood-prone areas.

(B) The forecast is for light to moderate showers to continue tonight.

(C) The Meteorological Service urged fishers to exercise caution as conditions could become life threatening.

(D) For further information, citizens can dial 116 or visit the website at http://metservice.gov.jm.

b Use your own words and information from the sources to explain what could happen in a flash flood. In your explanation give two examples, one example from **Source 1** and one from **Source 2**. For each example, include the source number.

Source 1 ____

Source 2 ____

Question 6

a Write some comments on how a flash flood can affect you in your home. Think of the different problems that may occur for you and your family, and what action you can take to help yourself and your family.

Problems	Solutions
Your home is located in a low-lying area that is prone to flooding.	
You are home alone when a flash flood warning is issued.	
Your family is separated during the flood.	
You are not allowed to leave your home during the flood.	
You may not have access to food, water or other necessities after the flood.	

Part 2

Be prepared!

Look at the writing prompt in question 7 and answer the questions below.

Question 7

Write a report advising people what to do if there is a flash flood warning when you are at home. Refer to your comments in question 6. Use text features such as the headings below or your own headings to organise your report.

- What is a flash flood?
- What are the signs of a flash flood?
- What should you do if you are at home and there is a flash flood warning?
- What are the dangers of flash floods?
- How can you stay safe during a flash flood?

Writing

Reflection

Use your answers to the task to analyse your strengths and weaknesses.

- What areas are you good at?
- Which areas require more work?
- What work will you do?

Practice paper 10

This task has 2 parts:

- Part 1 has 6 questions.
- Part 2 has 1 question.

For both parts, you must read **Source 1** and **Source 2**. Remember to read each question carefully, then answer all of them in each part in the spaces provided.

Part 1

Weathering the tropics

SOURCE 1

Hi John,

We have just returned from our two-week Caribbean holiday that I booked myself, although my parents booked the hotels themselves. So, we made all the reservations well in advance of the trip ourselves without using a travel agent. I think if you want something done properly, it is best you do it yourself, and I was right. The weather was glorious! We stayed in Jamaica for a week and then went to Cuba. The food was to die for! The sun was a bright golden yellow and shone brightly like a jewel in the sky almost every day. It was magical! I keep asking myself why I did not do this before. However, torrential rain occurred the day we travelled from Jamaica to Cuba. It was the heaviest rain in a thousand years! We were lucky because we were indoors at the airport and our flights were not delayed. The flight was bumpy like a fairground ride, but we arrived safely. When we got to Cuba we had flown out of the storm and into beautiful fine weather again. The hotel staff in Cuba were very friendly and there was a huge sign in the reception saying, "Make Yourselves at Home". We really enjoyed ourselves. Very different from the freezing winter weather we get in London!

Anne

SOURCE 2

A High Wind in Jamaica

The sun was still red and large: the sky above cloudless, and light blue glaze poured over baking clay: but close over the ground a dirty grey haze hovered. As they followed the lane towards the sea, they came to a place where, yesterday, a fair-sized spring had bubbled up by the roadside. Now it was dry. But even as they passed, some water splashed out, and then it was dry again, although gurgling inwardly to itself. But the group of children were hot, far too hot to speak to one another: they sat on their ponies as loosely as possible, longing for the sea. The morning advanced. The heated air grew quite easily hotter, as if from some enormous furnace from which it could draw at will. Bullocks only shifted their stinging feet when they could bear the soil no longer: even the insects were too lethargic to pipe, the basking lizards hid themselves and panted. It was so still you could have heard the least buzz a mile off. Not a naked fish would willingly move his tail. The ponies advanced because they must. The children ceased even to think.

Richard Hughes

Look at **Source 1**.

Question 1

a Who did Anne go on holiday with? Justify your answer.

b Anne wrote, “The food was to die for”. What did she mean?

c What was the weather like on Anne’s final day in Jamaica?

d Why were Anne and her travel companions lucky?

e On the day Anne arrived in Cuba, what was different about the weather in Jamaica compared to Cuba?

___

___

Question 2

a What was Anne's overall impression of her Caribbean holiday?

___

b What advice would Anne give to someone planning a Caribbean holiday?

___

Question 3

Who do the reflexive pronouns refer to in the following sentences from the letter?

a "… my parents booked the hotels themselves, …" ___

b "So, we made all the reservations well in advance of the trip ourselves …"

___

c "I keep asking myself why I did not do this before" ___

d "Make Yourselves at Home" ___

e "We really enjoyed ourselves" ___

Question 4

Read the letter again.

a Find two examples from the text that are facts.

___

___

b Find two examples from the text that are opinions.

____

____

c Anne uses similes (figurative language for dramatic effect). Write two examples of similes from the letter.

____

____

Look at **Sources 1** and **2**.

Question 5

a Which source is mainly about a holiday experience? ______________

b Describe two ways, one from each source, that the weather affects the characters' mood.

Source 1 ____

____

Source 2 ____

____

c What is the difference between the tone of **Source 1** and **Source 2**? Explain why, using examples from both sources.

____

____

____

d What are the features of **Source 1** and **Source 2** as text types?

____

____

e Which source do you think is more interesting or engaging to read? Explain why, using examples from both sources.

Question 6

Make some notes about your likes and dislikes about the Jamaican weather.

Consider these questions:

- Which weather conditions do you like/dislike? Why?
- What words describe those conditions?
- How do those conditions make you feel?
- Do you remember a particular experience that happened to you because of the conditions?

Like – Dream weather	**Dislike** – Nightmare weather
sunshine – glorious	hurricanes – windy
relaxing	terrifying
fun times – swimming, football	no electricity, lost our roof

Part 2

What's the weather like in Jamaica?

Question 7

Write an essay about what you like and dislike about the weather in Jamaica. You can add thoughts about your "dream" and/or "nightmare" weather. Your essay will be displayed on the class wall for others to read, so include some pleasant as well as some serious experiences. Make it entertaining!

- Use transitional words (first, in addition, consequently …) to help your sentences flow. Use similes to describe the conditions that you like and dislike. This will make your writing more exciting and vivid!
- Use the table and your comments in question 6 to help you.

ICT link: You could use Google Slides to create a short presentation about Jamaica's weather. Add pictures, transitions and simple sentences to show what you like and dislike.

Writing

Reflection

Use the table to rate your understanding of the Language Arts skills needed in this task.

My work shows that I ...	Rating
understand all of the Language Arts skills needed to complete this task.	4
understand most of the Language Arts skills needed to complete this task.	3
understand some of the Language Arts skills needed to complete this task.	2
have limited understanding of the Language Arts skills needed to complete this task.	1

Writing

Writing

Writing

Writing